# Ships
## and Boats

Written by
## Sally Hewitt and Nicola Wright

Designed by
## Chris Leishman

Illustrated by
## Rachael O'Neill

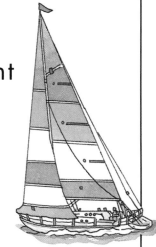

# Contents

# Afloat

All ships and boats, from giant supertankers to tiny rowing boats, have the same names for their different parts.

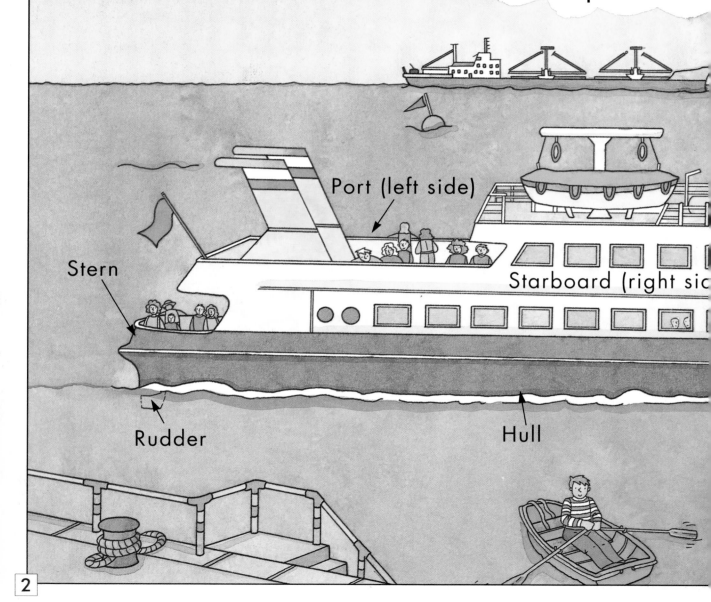

Port (left side)

Starboard (right si

Stern

Rudder

Hull

**Flyer Fun Fact**

Rich people who went to the Far East on the cool side of the ship were called **POSH** - because they travelled on the **P**ort side **O**ut and the **S**tarboard side **H**ome.

Bow

Anchor

**Engines** are used to drive ships and boats of all sizes.

**Sails** Sailing boats move along when the wind fills their sails.

**Oars and paddles** Rowers pull oars and paddles through the water to move their boats along.

3

# Ferries

Ferries carry passengers, cars, trucks and sometimes even trains on short journeys from port to port.

**Hovercraft**
Hovercraft ride just above the waves on a cushion of air.

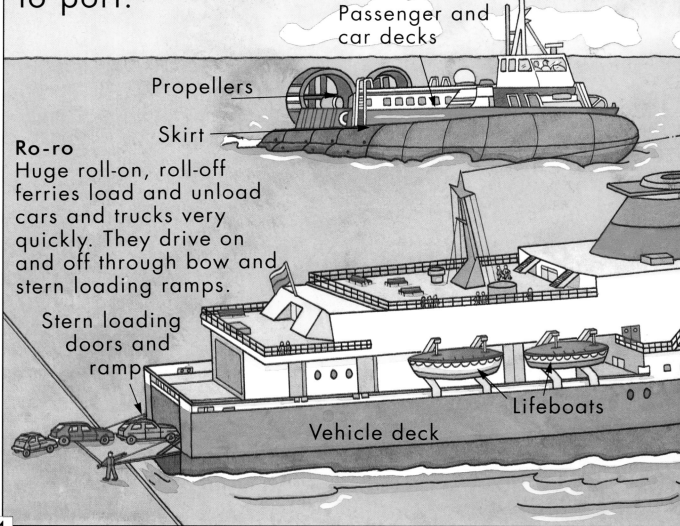

Passenger and car decks

Propellers

Skirt

**Ro-ro**
Huge roll-on, roll-off ferries load and unload cars and trucks very quickly. They drive on and off through bow and stern loading ramps.

Stern loading doors and ramp

Lifeboats

Vehicle deck

**Hydrofoil**
This ferry skims across the water on small, very strong wings called foils.

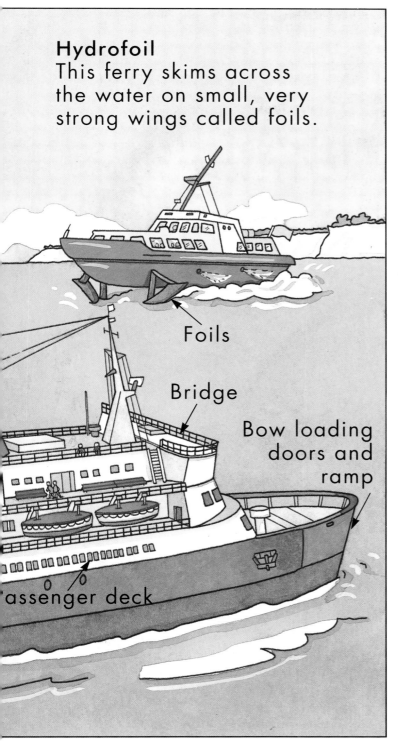

Foils

Bridge

Bow loading doors and ramp

Passenger deck

**Skirt** The hovercraft's skirt fills with air. It can ride on air over ground as well as on waves.

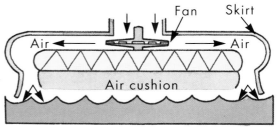

Fan    Skirt

Air    Air

Air cushion

**Foils** Foils are like aeroplane wings. Hydrofoils have to get up speed before they can 'take off'.

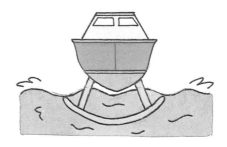

# Fishing

Fishing at sea can be a dangerous job. Fishermen often risk their lives in storms and freezing weather.

**Fish factory ship**
The catch is dropped onto a conveyor belt. Inside the ship the fish is cleaned, packed and frozen. It is often stored for weeks in a large refrigerated hold.

Winch

Ramp

Conveyer belt

## Trawler

Trawlers are usually small. The fish is packed in ice and only keeps fresh for about 14 days.

Refrigerated store

# Bringing in the catch

A net called a **trawl** is dragged through the water.

A **winch** hauls the trawl full of fish up the stern ramp.

The crew prepares the fish in safety on the **lower deck**.

# Floating hotels

Cruise ships are big floating hotels. Passengers travel in comfort to interesting places all over the world. There is plenty to do on board.

Swimming pools

Shops

Dance Floor

Library

Hospital

Cabins

Theatre

Lounge

**Flyer Fun Fact**

Passenger liners take about 3 days to cross the Atlantic. Concorde can fly from London to New York in under 4 hours!

**Bridge** The captain and officers control the ship from the bridge.

**Stabilizers** Small fins, called stabilizers, help to stop the ship rolling from side to side.

**Propellers** Powerful engines turn huge propellers which drive the ship through the water.

# Cargo carriers

Some ships are specially built to carry enormous amounts of cargo. They can carry loads for long distances, from country to country.

**Container ship**
Containers arrive at the port on trucks and trains. High-speed lifting cranes load them on to the container ship.

Moving crane

Containers

## Supertanker
This supertanker carries over 500,000 tonnes of oil in rows of tanks in its hull.

Tank hatches

Supertankers are too big for most harbours. Oil is loaded and unloaded in deep water through **pipes** into

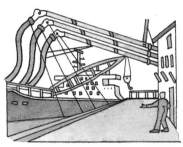

**smaller tankers** which carry the oil ashore.

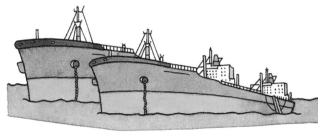

**Containers** are big boxes filled with cargo that stack neatly together.

# Warships

Different kinds of warships are designed to fight on the water, or underwater, or to help planes fight in the air.

## Aircraft carrier
Fighter planes and helicopters take off and land on aircraft carriers.

## Destroyer
Destroyers and cruisers armed with guns and missiles fight on the water.

# Submarines

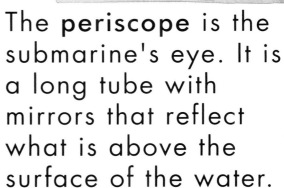

**Minesweeper**
Underwater explosives called mines are found and destroyed by minesweepers.

Submarines are ships that can travel under water. They carry special missiles, called torpedoes, which can be fired under water.

The **periscope** is the submarine's eye. It is a long tube with mirrors that reflect what is above the surface of the water.

# Ships for special jobs

Dredgers are used to move mud off the seabed near to the shore so ships do not get stuck. They are also used to collect building materials such as rocks.

Flyer Fun Fact

Mud dumped out at sea is nearly always washed back in again!

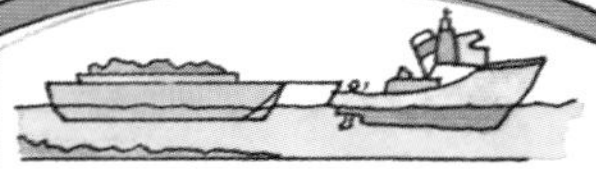

Buckets
Chute
Barge

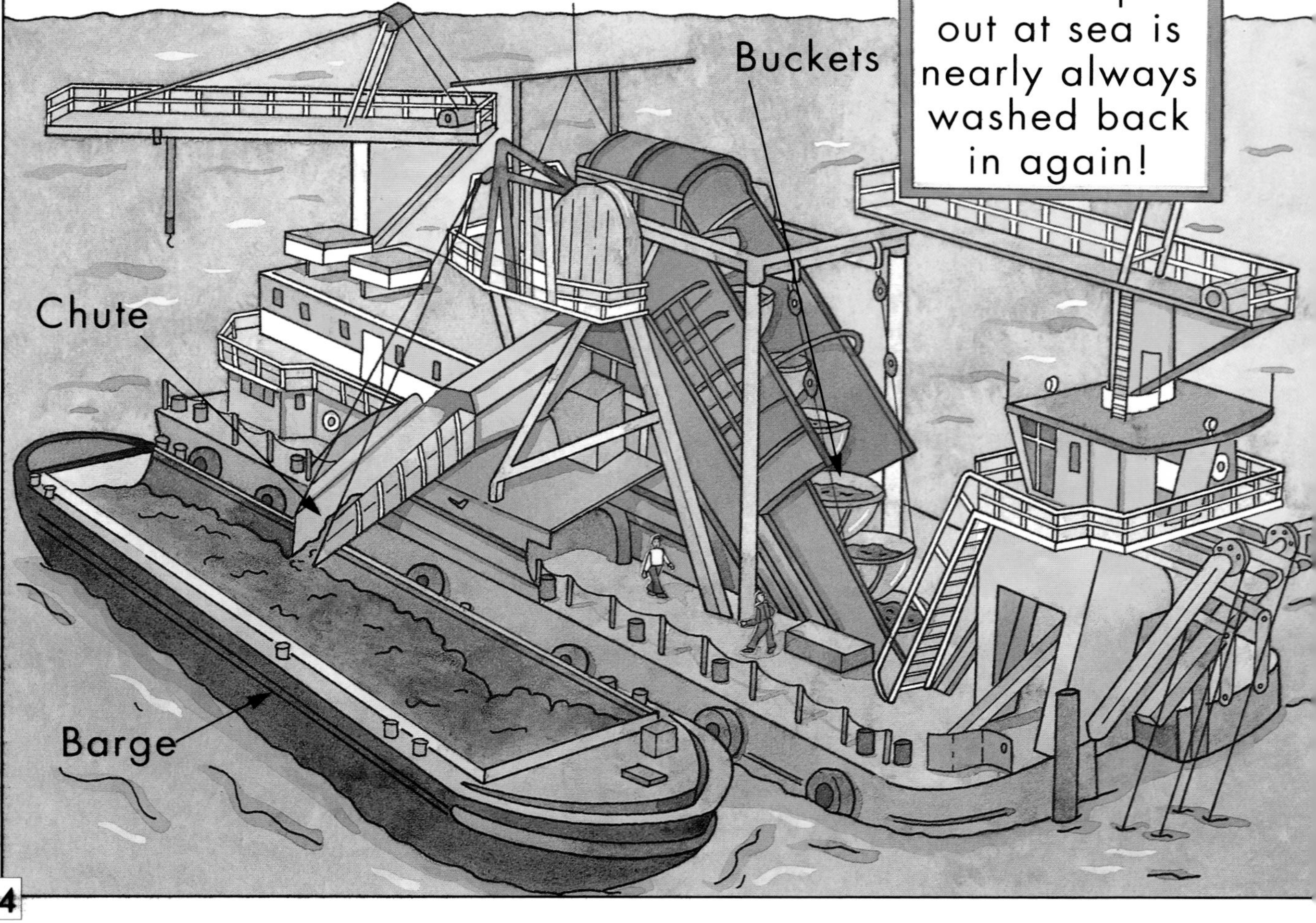

Icebreakers ride up onto the ice. The heavy bow breaks the ice. Then the extra-wide hull clears a wide path.

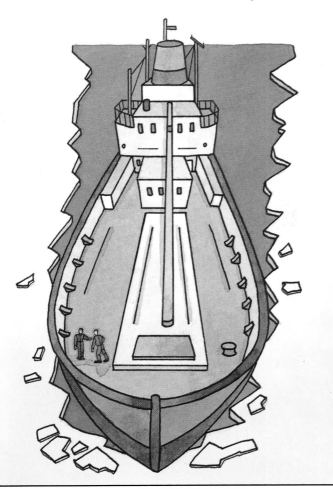

## Special features

Dredger **buckets** move round on a ladder scooping up mud. It slides down chutes into barges and is dumped further out to sea.

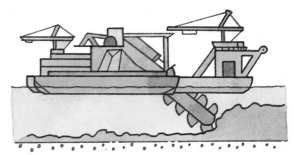

Some dredgers use pipes to suck up soft mud.

# Sailing

Sailing ships, boats and yachts catch the wind in their sails to move them along.

Sail

Forestay

Jib

Bow sprit

Shroud

**Dinghy**
One sail and a good wind is enough to speed this dinghy along.

Yard

Mast

Brace

Gaff

Boom

Rudder

**Tall ship**
This tall ship has 4 masts and 30 sails.

## Sails

Sails are attached to a tall pole called a **mast**.

The sail is stretched out onto a **boom** which can swing round to catch the wind.

The crew control the sail with a rope called a **sheet**.

17

# Speeding

Fast boats are built for racing and having fun, and also rescuing.

**Racing boat**
Racing boats have pointed bows and powerful engines.

**Cruiser**
You can eat, sleep and live in comfort on board a cruiser.

**Lifeboat**
Lifeboats are specially designed to stay afloat in very rough seas.

**Motorboat**
A motorboat can tow a waterskier.

**Outboard engines** are fitted on the outside of a boat. They can be taken on and off.

**Inboard engines** are built into a boat.

**Jet skis** are like motorbikes on water.

# Oars and paddles

Boats without engines or sails need human power to move them along.

Rowing boat

**Rowing eights**
Rowing eights are used for racing. The cox steers and shouts instructions to the crew.

**Kayak**
A kayak is a very light canoe.

## Methods

### One paddle

Canoeists hold one paddle with both hands. They push it into the water on either side of the canoe and pull back.

**Two oars can be used** on either side of a rowing boat.

### One oar

Using one oar at the back of the boat is called sculling.

# Finding the way

There are no roads and signposts at sea to help sailors. These are some of the things they use to help them find their way.

**Navigation lights**
A red port light and a green starboard light show the direction a ship is sailing in.

## Flyer Fun Fact
Sailors have always used the position of the stars and planets to find their way.

**Satellite**
Satellites send out signals that help ships to work out exactly where they are.

**Lighthouse**
Lighthouses mark harbour entrances and warn ships of dangerous rocks and tides.

**Buoy**
Floating marker buoys mark rocks and other dangers.

**Radar** shows where other ships and land are so ships can sail at night or in fog without colliding.

**Charts** are sea maps showing where dangerous rocks and sandbanks are.

A **compass** points to the North. Ships use them to work out which way to go.

# Index

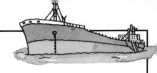

Edited by Nicola Wright and Dee Turner
Series concept: Tony Potter
Consultant: Robin Wright, M.M., M.A.
Design Manager: Kate Buxton
Colour separations by Scan Trans, Singapore
Printers: G Canale & Co SpA, Italy

This book was created by Zigzag Publishing Ltd, 5 High Street, Cuckfield, Sussex RH17 5EN, England

First published in Canada in 1993 by Zigzag Publishing Ltd

Copyright © Zigzag Publishing Ltd

ISBN 1 874647 09 7

10 9 8 7 6 5 4 3 2 1